Bridget Beth Collins

flora FORAGER
ABC

little bigfoot
an imprint of sasquatch books
seattle, wa

Look carefully in the garden
at the petals and leaves.
You can find animals in the flowers—
an alphabet menagerie!

Aa

Angelfish

Bb

Blue-footed booby

Cc

Camel

Dragon

Dd

Ee

Elephant

Ff

Fox

Gg

Giraffe

Hedgehog

Hh

Insect

I i

Jj

Jellyfish

Koala

Kk

L l

Leopard

Mm

Macaw

Nn

Narwhals

Oo

Owls

Pp

Piglet

Qq

Quail

Rr

Raccoon

Ss

Snakes

Tt

Turtle

Uu

Unicorn

Vv

Vampire bat

W
W

Woodpeckers

Xerus inauris
(Cape ground squirrel)

X x

Yak

Yy

Zebra

Zz

For Finn,
Oliver, and Harry

Manufactured in China by C&C Offset Printing Co. Ltd.
Shenzhen, Guangdong Province, in June 2022

LITTLE BIGFOOT with colophon is a registered
trademark of Penguin Random House LLC

26 25 24 23 22   10 9 8 7 6 5 4

Editor: Christy Cox
Production editor: Nicole Burns-Ascue
Design: Bryce de Flamand
Copyeditor: Em Gale

Library of Congress Cataloging-in-Publication Data

Names: Collins, Bridget Beth, author.
Title: Flora Forager ABC / Bridget Beth Collins.
Description: Seattle, WA : Little Bigfoot, an imprint of Sasquatch Books,
    [2019]
Identifiers: LCCN 2018014485 | ISBN 9781632172099 (hardcover)
Subjects: LCSH: Animals--Juvenile literature.
Classification: LCC QL49 .C6735 2018 | DDC 590--dc23
LC record available at https://lccn.loc.gov/2018014485

ISBN: 978-1-63217-209-9

Sasquatch Books
1325 Fourth Avenue, Suite 1025
Seattle, WA 98101

SasquatchBooks.com